Le [...]
un cour[...]
    dessin,
une femme très passionnée!
        Heather Spears.

Magnifique!

# REQUIRED READING

A witness in words and drawings to
The Reena Virk Trials 1998-2000

# REQUIRED READING

A witness in words and drawings to
The Reena Virk Trials 1998-2000

by Heather Spears

WOLSAK AND WYNN  •  TORONTO

Typeset in Garamond, printed in Canada by
The Coach House Printing Company, Toronto.

Cover image: © Heather Spears
Cover design: The Coach House Printing Company
Author's photograph: Thorndahl, Copenhagen
All drawings © Heather Spears, published with the consent of The Canadian
Press and CHEKTV. The portrait of Reena Virk is published with the
consent of Tarseem Pallan.

We wish to express our gratitude to the Canada Council for the Arts and the
Ontario Arts Council for supporting our publishing program.

Wolsak and Wynn Publishers Ltd.
Post Office Box 316
Don Mills, Ontario
Canada M3C 2S7


CANADIAN CATALOGUING IN PUBLICATION DATA

Spears, Heather, 1934-
  Required Reading

ISBN 0-919897-70-3

1. Virk, Reena, 1983-1997 – Poetry. 2. Trials (Murder) – British Columbia
– Vancouver – Poetry. I. Title.

PS8537.P4R46 2000     C811'.54     C00-932441-0
PR9199.3.S6314R46 2000

*for Reena*

# Contents

# Introduction

Since 1998 I have followed the Reena Virk Trials as a courtroom artist. These trials, though generally called by the name of this child, are characterized by her absence: they are the trials of her schoolmates and contemporaries, who swarmed her, beat her, and, in the case of two of them, were convicted of killing her.

Why did I draw? I work very seldom as a court artist, only if a case interests me, and then it is usually in the range of my obsessions as an artist – children in crisis, children as victims, and, yes, this time children as perpetrators. I wanted to go deeply into this in order to finish with it, come out at the other side. I have made over 500 drawings and, while working, have not consciously judged or pre-judged, trying to be there as an attentive witness through my art to what I have seen.

So this is not a complete record; it is as impersonal as I could make it but it is personal.

I was to make a presentation of the drawings with poems, and was booked to do so even as the trials dragged on. I realized I had no poems, so they were written in haste, long before I would usually write anything to resolve a series of drawings. They are more of a piece with the drawings themselves, and there was no tranquillity in the writing of them. This text, though it may raise questions and discussion, does not give any answers.

Those who have followed the case already know that Reena Virk lived part of the time in care, and had called her family to say that she was coming home for a visit. Two of her schoolmates had planned to give her a beating for the supposed taking of an address book and phoning around – one witness said it was because "Reena was saying she was going out with people she wasn't and sleeping with people she wasn't."

That night of November 14, 1997, she was enticed to the Gorge waterway, a beautiful narrow inlet in Victoria, near the school, and there savagely set upon. Most of the children then left her and she staggered across the wooden bridge; but two followed her and drowned her in the Gorge. The two convicted of the murder were the then 15-year-old Warren Glowatski, and Kelly Ellard, who had also just turned 15.

Rumours spread quickly, the perpetrators were soon arrested, and the body found. The children's code of "not ratting out" made for a tangle of lies and partial evidence but the general thread was certain. Five girls were convicted of the swarming. As juvenile offenders, they cannot be named. I was allowed to draw them but their faces may not be shown. Warren Glowatski and Kelly Ellard were tried and convicted separately in adult court.

A note on the text: The title refers to the second poem, the "required reading" being the objective "reading" of the wounds by the pathologist and, in parallel, my act of witnessing through drawing. "The Adidas jacket" refers to the jacket Reena was wearing when she was attacked. "In camera": Warren, who was convicted and jailed in 1999, refused to testify at the 2000 trial of Kelly Ellard. The poems are followed by an epilogue by my niece, Holly Spears, which gives another perspective.

## The besetting

1
"It was a besetting"
says the judge
using the old Germanic word
"vicious, childishly premeditated, cruel"
*besat* the passive means possessed
as by demons.  Which it almost was:
"Every time we kicked her
she'd puke blood" that kind of thing.
Accelerated past spitefulness
or even pleasure – "I don't know why" they said –
as if in themselves they were inhabited.

2
Easier to explain then than now
why Reena went to the ground
though the young girls
(*parties, principals, aiders and abetters*)
would have been much the same
except more roughly clothed, more rudely
benched
no modern need to understand
the deed, not then, no argument, they'd have
been
summarily dispatched
with their unseen and desperate familiars.

A lawyer is talking in the hallway
he sends his daughter to karate
she will not be a victim
she will grow up "able to fight back."

## Required reading

1
This is required reading
the slab, the sluiced floor
no one hasn't been there
every murder film or story
gives you the cool pathologist
funny or otherwise
sawing sorting picking through
it's part of the plot,
expected, necessary.  It's not
the drama proper, it's not
action it's aftermath
it's the detachment
that hooks you, she pulls on
gloves, her hands
move in, but as if they were
attached to her like tools, metal or silicone,
at a distance and without
involvement if ever so careful
ever so sure.  I know
this act, this silence, I have also done
this kind of thing.

15

2

Not violence but the remains
of violence, the remains
of what was before violence which means
a healthy, living child, intact
tissues, a steady pounding heart
details like the black
hair on her lower back
formed in a crown, as if repeatedly combed.
The vulnerable perfect
corner of her lips, or the prophetic
colour of her lips — a dashed vermilion.
Now swollen, spread, and every bruise
meticulously witnessed and written down
under the pitiless light.

3

You said it, pitiless, it has to be,
in order to see it, these hands
made light of these terrible things
because they had to, someone did
because it was required
the enumeration of the wounds
a kind of secular
stations of the cross, she got up she fell
here she was struck here she clung
to a railing here she covered her head
or tried to, here she crawled
such and such a distance, here they returned
here were delivered
so many kicks or about so many
and here
she did not move, but was moved

down a slope of grass
described as "slippery"
while the judge remarked we do not need
an expert witness to tell us
grass is slippery after rain.
You go through it
knowing how it's going to end
as if you were in a church but your beads
are words and each word
passes between your fingers and there is nothing
you did not expect to hear
you have to get through it and
you know it happened
and even this close
it's turning into a story.

20

## The footstool

Reena's grandmother
has a small embroidered stool
carved all about
which every day she carries into court
on which she places her feet
it came from the Old Country
it is innocent, though it has been
here and there, in the quietness
of living rooms, at all the celebrations
each grandchild handed over it and held
it has been at gatherings after funerals

where she would sit down
on the best chair, arrange her white
sari, surreptitiously remove her shoes
and place her bare feet
and look about her, unhurried, benevolent
in the bosom of her family
this is getting maudlin

no one expected it, or her bare feet or her look
to end up here.

23

## Court followers

1
Familiar now among the crowd
outside the courtroom closing in
on Reena's family
grabbing a bench behind them when we get in
a woman with a wild look and faded hair
and a sheaf of notes
writing with all her might
she's under directives, voices
she alone can hear, she knows
the trial depends on her, its imperious outcome
she leans she inserts herself the family
endure her as they endure the rest
she can do them no further harm

I think if I spoke
to her once I would become her
it's that close so I keep
my distance
I have a feeling there is no difference between us, none
what am I doing here?

2

And here comes the other woman, loud, stout,
utterly without
reserve or courtesy
who has fastened on them, scurries
to them, swells herself, prepared to defend
against all comers.  Whose plump hand
when the blows are being described
pats at the mother's shoulders
who in the breaks
buys candy for the little sister
stares (as they do not) fiercely about
wades right in
with her comfort and indignation –
human, lowest common denominator
human – why not?  Is she worse
than the rest of us?
*Good Hope, Desolation* –
as the port is named for the storm.

**Warren then**

There are pleas of depression
small stature, immaturity
the alcoholic mother the divorce
quarrels he did not understand
shutting himself in his room
whatever that world is
he has to find out now, before his time
raised to adult court
for the severity of the crime.

At his arrest
he was overheard on the phone
shouting to his dad who was not there:
"I'm fucked for the rest of my life."

a photograph of the
body in the water

29

**In the dock**

1
The sheriff with the cropped hair
is in place at the gate
into the dock, she's gamin her perked hip
drips with the approved junk – holster, phone, slung keys
her tough look
exaggerated, as in a farce, pleased to be
playing herself.

And now they bring him in
he is the shorter, at her side
seems almost more the girl but it's a close thing
behind his back she unlocks
his handcuffs and without thinking he bends
head and shoulders forward to give her space
two kids in a game
this can't be serious.

31

2

If it's serious why
is he hiding? Through the whole
arraignment he's crouched down in the box
and only his light hair
shows, his narrow T-shirt shoulders
while the voices drone on
and the dossiers are paged and turned and filed
and nobody cracks a smile
bobbing for the judge
*my respectful submission*
*my learned friend*
and *if it please*
and *your honour must disabuse his mind* –

Tiered, windowless the room
preserves its hierarchies, invites the eye
upward to the judge's seat, the high-
backed chair
and over him on the wall
*Dieu et mon Droit* the lion
rampant etc. it's all
so formal except for the child
whose posture they're somehow
managing to ignore
no one, I am fairly sure
ever did this before.

3

Was he then
afraid of our looks, of every eye
fastened on him, the fascination
the harm in it?  Enough to hide
inside the panels that support the glass
the way at a Victorian trial
the accused beautiful woman was
allowed to faint away –
does he think this has to be OK?
The sheriff stands there so alert
ready to grab him should he really fall
forward and do himself an injury.
Her lips part in her hard little face, her look
has softened almost into pity.

35

When he came in I know
he saw what I was up to
but what difference can it make
this invasion, whether he's drawn or only seen?
Everyone's stare
must hurt him equally. It can't be me
I am nearly sure.

## Witness

Tall, plausible, the one
who did not implicate himself
who only intervened
once, to pull Warren away
"Cool it, it's not your fight"
he said and only circumstance
prevented a second stepping-in
when his girlfriend who said "I don't like fights"
felt sick (later a witness,
she threw up in the hall
giggled on the stand)
so he'd left with her to take her home.
Which may or may not be true.

39

Freely he lied for Warren
without stint without shame,
at the station, at the arraignment –
"You lied to protect your friend."
"Yeah."  Now with the pointer he
traces the bridge the infamous innocent stairs
where Reena slumped at the rail
where "her head jolted with each kick."
"Even now," he's told, "You're finding it hard
to sell your buddy down the river."
He says his present statements are consistent.
He has short hair.
Across that distance
he explains
as to a foreigner,
"You don't rat out on a friend."
Then like an afterthought:
"If you do, you have to watch your back."

41

**The sweetheart**

Round face round-eyed
being made to tell
in his presence (she is in the stand
he is in the dock she does not look)
how he knelt and held her hands
in his hands and asked
if she knew what it meant, the rap
*One eighty-seven*, which is police for homicide –
and he said "exactly that."
And now she has bad dreams
she is not involved
except by what he said.

"He has burdened you
with the knowledge of murder.
This is as serious as it gets."

45

## Disembodied

He is so small
only his head is visible
rides over the gate
like some swimmer in standing water.
Even his nape and chin
hid by the dock.
"Disembodied" wrote *The Times-Colonist*
a happy choice.

It's no good for me I need
the source, the how of him
the frown of his shoulders the head stem's
emergence from its roots
deep in his heart's unfailing chambers
I need the way he simply puts his hands
on his knees, or folds his arms
the way his chest breathes (
he is one of those (they are so rare)
who never touch their face.

And now his lightless look
flits across mine
what does he see?  I hope only my emptiness
where I attend, attend
behind the shame of my intent.

49

**Kelly then**

1

What was I at nearly 15, can I even remember
the stance and simmering, the way
at that age I walked, ran, lay down
every night my bare feet
pressed into the cold of the sheets
healthy sleep and my eyes
opening into the next day
with or without residual
fear?  For her it is already
nearly three years ago, can she
remember, I saw her then
at the arraignment, in profile
a kid in a pony tail,
lower lip stubborn and downcast eyes –
anger or heedlessness?  She was not

casual like the others, the ones
who'd swarmed and punched and left it at that
she went back
of course in the court the others
had each other, were brought in
in twos and threes, the defence
spoke to them like pals
hands in his pockets, rocking on his heels
used what he took for teenage slang
*you guys, hanging out*, etc.
and gave them to understand
(as he must, in giving the judge to understand)
that what they did
was no big deal.  Dangerous.

51

52

And they crossed their legs, examined their nails
loosened their long hair
from their collars in gestures that appeared
bored and disdainful.  Were given
yellow foolscap and pens, and expected to write
to appear attentive at least
as if they were in school
but they did not know what to write
and were not asked to speak
and were charged.  Their friends
in baseball caps came in to see
no one expressed very much
a few tears at the end
for the sentencing I think, not for Reena
I think this is true
though I have no way to know what is true
except my eyes, my attention
beyond that
I can't be sure.

2

But she was on her own
and is so still and what they say she did
took the whole thing
into another dimension —
now at 17, isolate, is she the same
she will have changed and grown
and whether her heart changed, or was changed,
is anybody's guess.
I haven't seen her yet,
I haven't yet gone in.  Old events
dictate this, old images still hold, over a new emergent face.

57

**Kelly now**

is different of course
almost a woman, anonymous
as the cover photo on a magazine
nothing there
but low-key glamour and gloss her hair
nicely cut swings to hide her look
her clothes in dark gray and black
and nothing to pin on, no quirk or frown
plain clean the way she stands up, sits down
they could have put
anyone there to take her place
(everyone's saying it: "the girl next door")
neither short nor tall
from where I sit I just can't see her face.

When they began to show
the Saanich video of her arrest
over two years ago
her head inched down
maybe an inch into her collar, that was all.

she was asking me why I was wearing high heels (tape)

60

**The soft room**

At Saanich police station
they've set aside a room –
"Normally," a sergeant says, "there's stuffed animals
there's a love seat
it's used to interview children
in cases of child abuse (
( It's known as the soft room"
*a love seat*
*normally*
the video is bad the black
machine swivelled at the judge so the tiny heads
of mother and girl elongate, dull curtains a lot
of static and flack
and now the prosecutor lifts her arm, aims the remote
fast forwards while the sleeve
of her gown widens and after a silence
the inanimate voices resume,
one childish one a man's
hours of it
"You are being charged
with murder do you understand?"
This is *the soft room*
"I didn't do anything.
I wanna go home."
This is *normally*.

**The smoke pit**

What Kelly said at the smoke pit
the place by Shoreline
where the smokers hang out
spread fast around the school
I didn't believe it, I thought it was a joke
but that afternoon
she took me to Craigflower schoolhouse
and there were Reena's shoes
lined up on the steps, and then
we walked by the Gorge, and she told
me to help look for clothes in the water.
"I was curious, and she was willing to tell me."
She said they went back to see
if Reena was all right she said
they had to break Reena's ams
so she wouldn't swim away
and she held her down and he did it. She said
they "sat there and pretty much watched
for about 45 minutes" and
he said they should finish her off
because if they didn't she'd rat
and they'd be in lots of
trouble.

## The line search

"The tide was in flood
moving up the Gorge Waterway
… visibility at most three feet
you go along four inches at a time
using your hands and your eyes –
the usual trash, bottles and shells –
in the eel grass below you could see the band
of a pair of underwear –"
Then her jeans – "they were fastened, the button
was done up –"
the police diver, solid and erect,
his hands clasped over his paunch
("I prefer to stand")
speaks straightforwardly
being used to this but even so
his words become a kind of poem.

Sergeant John Archer

"There was a thin layer of silt on the ocean floor –
Light through water diffuses – the cloth
was a light, grayish green –"
then "we observed the body in the water
face down head down, round shoulders,
arms straight down, legs hanging
what we referred to as a child
as the *jelly fish float* –

"She was very hard to the touch, no
elasticity – the term we use
is *saponification* – a process the body goes through –
the skin solidifies – the fat I should say –"

The courtroom returns with the funny word,
the press all trying to hear, trying to spell
glancing aside into each other's papers
( here is no poem after all
he is handed jeans in a plastic bag
to identify – "that is correct" –
turns and holds out one silty cuff:
"There is still some eel grass on it, see –"
*eel grass*

71

## The pathologist

The pathologist too
cannot but speak in pictures
it is her method to be plain
"The skull was very soft and boggy."
"The tissues were sheared."
Between sessions she stands
outside the glass doors in the rain
for a smoke her hands
are beautiful
remember in the court her palm,
to demonstrate, placed
against her close-cropped head

and how she touched her throat
"The thorax was crushed against the spine."
she is asked what "stomping" means and says
"a blow with the sole of a piece of footwear."
She is not theatrical
the quiet gesture of the wrist the unalterable word
remote, as if she were still on the far side
of glass. "Reena was alive
when she went into the water."  Question:
"And what if she had not been drowned?"
Answer: "I believe she would have died."

**The Adidas jacket**

Erna in purple testifies:
"I had just dropped Robbie off at the longhouse" she says
his jacket had been lost some days before.
So when she saw one
"hanging on a white picket fence"
she turned the car
but by then it was gone and she saw
a jogger with something rolled under her arm
("To be perfectly honest I don't know why
I chased that jogger down")
who relinquished it and said
she was giving it to the Sally Ann
anyway
and went on jogging.

"When I went to wash it
it was covered in blood all down the front.
Something sort of clicked and I thought O my God."

75

**In camera**

In camera, Warren has refused
twice to take the oath, stands
with hands held down and clasped tight
in front of his crotch
he's taller now
his voice soft still boyish
his look devoid of light
murmurs that if he testified he'd be hurt
in prison, perhaps killed it's happened then it's happening
the beginning of being
fucked for the rest of his life

cited for contempt of court
because of refusal to be sworn / to testify.
(remanded) 14 April 10 AM

**Kelly restless**

Now it begins
tweaks her hair
pulls one strand
nowhere to stare
nothing to do
looks up looks down
she's alive I'm reminded
I made another drawing then
she's the same one now
she's not
big curvy closer to
the size that Reena was and never a word
about the press till someone
wrote about "fat thighs" –
then she complained.

Running cameras caught
her face in the entrances
grim with endurance or
averted ducking into the car
they took one video
then ran the stills till they found
a twisted smirk which really was
only the fleeting change
between expressions
it's in all the papers
"Say did you see that photo?"
says an eager old man
suddenly in the hall
"It tells everything!"

80

I keep getting this picture of
the other one, the child
wading staggering thigh deep
skinny small fast the rush –
her laughter –
what's left?  I guess
this could be called
restless the way she moves around in court
but compared to then
it's slower, large, loopy, dreaming –
that was restless, then.

82

## Deliberation

Some are saying "home free" and some
"It could go either way"
and the grandfather, quietly:
"It doesn't matter any more."
I am left scared
I admit I have not presumed
innocence, I am unfair,
it never entered my head.

"God knows," says the grandmother
almost complacently.
Meaning that God knows.
Her hand on my arm.  The afternoon sun
soaks the rug, the red plush on the chairs
the fakelike ivy in its concrete troughs.
Lawyers scoot past, immaculate
as in films.  Near the door
the dowdy followers huddle, hum insistently,
try not to lose momentum.
Everything's suspended.
I have slept badly and doze,
sitting upright, start awake with a sense of dread.
People think she'll get off.

**For the defence**

Warren's lawyers pause, their gowns
swirl and settle as they bend
toward him over the rail and for once
he focusses his eyes
outward, past his despair, becomes
for a moment ordinary.

And Kelly's lawyer is treading to and fro
arms balled beneath his gown, scowling
with concentration.
I'm on the watch, I want to draw
him with her but he won't meet her eye.
Only after the verdict –
the court emptied the press
scrambling over each others' knees
to make the news – at last he goes
to her, enters the dock, sits down
embraces her absently he is still
staring forward as she dabs her eyes the noise
of her half sister weeping behind me their cell
phone
ringing ( someone saying "Yes…yes"
in a dead voice – so her own tears
are, if not unheard of,
unheard.

31.03.00

## The colour of right

This girl "had what adults call
*a colour of right,*
a belief that Reena had something in her bag."
The judge is summing up –
her pathetic bag, with the lipstick the perfume
the pyjamas for the visit home
the cigarettes everyone shared
before they tossed it empty over the bridge

*The colour of right* it's new to me
maybe I misheard
Reena who wanted with all her might
to belong, to be as she believed them light-
hearted, contemptuous, sarcastic, strong –
what she might have done
phoning around, pretending
to be important was foolish, maybe mildly wrong
but what happened was unfathomable,
edgeless, the wet slope
the underside of a bridge
mud and darkness
no safe hold
once opened it fell forever
no more colour then.

## Epilogue

### *Witness seat*
by Holly Spears

I chose a seat in the third row. I could see the witness stand and the defence attorney clearly. I sat in the same row as Reena's grandparents. I recognized them from the nightly news. They were there for Reena, to see that her life was vindicated. My eyes would not linger too long. To imagine what they felt and what they saw as they scanned the room was unbearable. Several teenage girls filled the seats behind me. They had glossy lips, and braces on their teeth. Were they there to support the defendant? If so, how did they wrap their young minds around this course of events? Had they all been there the night Reena had died? Had they seen her blood or heard her tears? Could they not have smelled her fear? I shift in my seat, nervous about who may sit beside me, whose arm might brush up against mine accidentally. Two old women sit front row, centre. They have foreign accents, German maybe. They are not associated with the defendant, the counsel, or the victim. Why are they here? Entertainment? Boredom? Or morbid fascination? Why am I here?

My aunt enters the courtroom, artist, poet, teacher. She opens her sketchbook and starts sketching furiously, hoping her drawings will sell for the six o'clock news or tomorrow morning's paper. Is this accused child killer the subject of art? She does not pose but keeps her eyes straight ahead. The first witness of the morning is brought in through a door hidden behind the judge's bench. She is wearing the customary blue sweatshirt that is reserved for those in youth custody. She is seventeen. I don't remember her name but her face is etched in my mind, an image that disturbs my own memory of what seventeen looked like.

The witness has a long criminal record that is relayed to the jury, establishing her as a teen prone to lying and violence. She admits to beating Reena, throwing punches during an unprovoked attack. Her answer to the question why is "I don't know." The image in my brain of the vicious attack makes me squirm in my seat. I do not look down the row at Reena's grandparents, I only imagine the pain and rage they must feel. I examine the witness for signs of remorse, fear, or horror at what she did and what she saw. There is nothing to see in her face or her eyes. Her eyes are blank and her face is hostile.

I can hear the scratching of my aunt's pencil. There is no way to draw the lack of conscience this child possesses. An assaulter of children, killer of youth, and witness for the crown is not art. Why does the concept of what she saw, what she did, not torment her? Does it haunt her only in her dreams or not at all? Is she at peace when awake, sitting here in the same room as Reena's grandparents?

I realize that the only presence I can understand in the courtroom is my own. I try to focus on my body but I only become aware of how painfully I need to use the washroom. My mind cannot absorb what it is hearing: this is reality and not a TV screen that I can scream and shout at. A very small part of me is actually present; mostly I am lost in a wave of youthful memories and teenage pains that cannot even be measured against the reality being presented in this room. The first break in the morning is a relief as I realize how tense my shoulders are and how hard my head is throbbing.

My aunt already has her drawings strewn across a table outside the courtroom by the time I have fought my way out. She is adding colour from her collection of pencil crayons. I watch her fill in the witness's face in flesh tones.

It seems unnatural on this girl's skin, the colour of flesh. I excuse myself to use the washroom. I end up walking down several floors of the courthouse to avoid any contact with the teenagers who sat behind me in the courtroom. I don't know whether I am frightened of them or not, but I am aware they make me uncomfortable.

Lunch break. I again catch up with my aunt outside. She is in a rush to get to the newspaper office during the one-hour recess. "Heavy morning," she says to me and all I can do is nod in reply. I tell her I am going home and she gives me a hug. Home – my place of refuge and safety. As we walk away from courtroom 54 I take one glance back at Reena's grandparents but there are no words that can express what I feel for them. There are no words to express how I feel about myself or even my world. Everything has shifted and turned upside-down in the last three hours. All that is left are questions with no answers.

At home I imagine Reena's body lying at the bottom of the Gorge. All the blood has washed away and her bones have delicately fused back together. She is perfect. Youthful wings stretch and envelop her. She is carried out to the sea, flying freely.

**Other books by Heather Spears:**

Asylum Poems (1958)
The Danish Portraits (1967)
From the Inside (1972)
Drawings from the Newborn (1986)
How to Read Faces (1986)
The Word for Sand (1988)
Human Acts (1991)
The Moonfall Trilogy (1992 – 1996)
The Panum Poems (1996)
Poems Selected and New (1998)